NINJA KID 4

AMAZING NINJA!

Scholastic Press
An imprint of Scholastic Australia Pty Limited (ABN 11 000 614 577)
PO Box 579 Gosford NSW 2250
www.scholastic.com.au

Part of the Scholastic Group
Sydney • Auckland • New York • Toronto • London • Mexico City
• New Delhi • Hong Kong • Buenos Aires • Puerto Rico

First published by Scholastic Australia in 2019.

A catalogue record for this book is available from the National Library of Australia

Typeset in Bizzle-Chizzle, featuring Hola Bisou and Handblock.

ISBN 978-93-5471-834-2
First edition: 2019
This reprint edition: November 2025
Printed in India at MicorPrints India, New Delhi

ANH DO

illustrated by Jeremy Ley

NINJA KID 4

AMAZING NINJA!

A Scholastic Press book
from Scholastic Australia

ONE

My name is **Nelson Kane.** Until I turned ten, I was a skinny, unfit

NERD.

Then on my **tenth** birthday, I woke up with **amazing NINJA** skills! Now I'm

I inherited my ninja powers from my **dad.** He mysteriously **disappeared** when I was really young.

I live with my **mum,** Cousin **Kenny** and **Grandma Pat** on a **junkyard** in **Duck Creek.**

My grandma is an inventor. She never gives up.

That's just as well, because her inventions don't always turn out the way she imagined.

Like her flying clothes pegs. They're great when they do what they're **supposed** to . . .

But **terrible** when they get it **wrong**!

When Grandma's inventions do work, they're **OUT OF THIS WORLD!**

When I become **NINJA KID,** Kenny turns into **H-DUDE!**

H-Dude doesn't have any special powers but he is the **best sidekick** any ninja could ever have!

Other than Mum and Grandma, no-one else knows about our secret identities. But there is one man desperate to find out -

Andrew is my dad's twin brother. When they turned ten, Andrew was upset he didn't inherit the skills of a ninja like my dad did.

His jealousy turned into **ANGER** and a thirst for **POWER**.

Now Dr Kane wants to scare everyone **out of Duck Creek!**

So far, Dr Kane has unleashed **giant mutant spiders . . .**

He created an **e-virus** that caused all the animals to escape from the zoo . . .

He even came to our **athletics carnival** in disguise and tried to **capture** the best athletes. He was sure one of them would be Ninja Kid!

Luckily, we haven't seen Dr Kane in a while, which means Kenny and I can just be regular kids.

Regular kids who are **super excited** about **THE CIRCUS** coming to town!

I love everything about the circus.

The **animals . . .**

The **trapeze** artists . . .

The **Wheel of Steel!**

From the second our PE teacher, **Ms Quick,** told us we were going on an excursion to the circus, it was all we could talk about!

Ms Quick is one of my favourite teachers. Her name suits her perfectly . . . she's quicker than a **cheetah on rollerskates!**

A week before our excursion, we had PE class in the school gym.

'I have an exciting announcement to make,' Ms Quick said. 'The **SHAW FAMILY CIRCUS** is giving some lucky locals a chance to be **part of the show!**'

We all went **ballistic!**

'**Auditions** for the special performance will be held in **three days,**' Ms Quick said. 'So, **choose a partner** and start working out a **routine!**'

Before Kenny moved to my school, I used to hate it when a teacher asked us to choose a partner. I always seemed to be the one **left out.**

But now I don't have to worry because Kenny and I do everything together.

'Nelson . . .' Kenny said.

'You don't have to ask, Kenny, of course I'll be your partner!' I said.

'Actually, I was hoping to pair up with Tiffany . . .' Kenny said.

'Oh.'

For the first time in ages, I had that **sinking feeling** again.

'And one other thing,' Kenny said. 'Can you ask her for me?'

'I think it's better if you ask her yourself, Kenny!'

But Kenny had already run away and hidden behind the vaulting horse!

I wandered over to Tiffany. She didn't seem too interested in choosing a partner - she was focused on doing a crazy **backbend!**

'Ah, hi, Tiffany, how are you going down there?' I asked.

'Hi, Nelson!' Tiffany said, straightening up.

'So . . . Kenny wants to know if you'll be his partner for the auditions.'

'Love to! But why didn't Kenny ask me himself?'

'Ah . . . he's too busy practising on the vaulting horse . . .'

Tiffany looked across to Kenny, who quickly pretended he was doing gymnastics.

'Kenny's so funny!' Tiffany said. Then she went back to practising her backbends.

As I walked away, Kenny hurried over to me. 'What did she say?' he asked.

'Yes!' I replied.

'Yes!' Kenny exclaimed. He did a weird **star jump** to celebrate!

Now I had to find my own partner. I really wanted to ask **Sarah.**

Sarah is the **kindest** girl in our class.

She's always *nice* to everyone!

Just as I was about to talk to Sarah, **Charles Brock** pushed in front of me.

Charles Brock is the biggest bully at school. He is also the Mayor's son.

'Excuse me, Sarah,' Charles said. 'Would you do me the honour of being my circus audition partner?'

WHAT THE?! I had **NEVER** heard Charles speak politely before!

My **heart** was in my mouth as I waited for Sarah's reply. (Not actually in my mouth - that would be weird!)

It seemed like an **eternity** before Sarah finally responded. 'Um . . . sure, Charles, I'll try out for the circus with you,' she said.

I couldn't believe it! My heart hit the floor like a **dropped tomato.**

Charles's politeness didn't last long. '**Booyah!** Cop that, Nelson!' he said as he strutted away from Sarah.

'Alright, everyone, attention please,' Ms Quick called out to our class.

Kenny went to stand next to Tiffany. Sarah moved next to Charles.

'OK, has anyone **not** got a partner?' Ms Quick asked.

I was **Sooooo embarrassed.** The whole gym was **staring** at me.

Kenny waved his hand in the air. 'Ms Quick, can we have **three** in our group?' he asked.

'Yeah, we'd love to have Nelson join us,' Tiffany added.

'Excellent idea!' Ms Quick replied.

Suddenly, I didn't feel so terrible. Doing a routine with Kenny and Tiffany would be great.

After PE, Sarah raced over to me. 'Nelson, I was going to ask you to be my partner but I saw you talking to Tiffany and thought you'd already paired up with her. That's why I said yes to Charles.'

'**HEY!** Stop talking to the **enemy**, Sarah!' Charles called out. 'Some of his **hopelessness** might rub off on you!'

He really was back to his **bullying** self.

'You're **not the boss** of me, Charles,' Sarah replied. She turned to me again. 'Next time we're asked to pair up for something, you can ask me if you want to, OK?'

'Deal!' I replied.

My **heart leapt** off the floor and **jumped** back into my chest!

TWO

Kenny and I were used to arriving home from school to find Grandma doing **something bizarre.**

Like the time we got home and Grandma was trying out her flying armchair!

This time, we found Grandma wearing a huge silver helmet and **talking to a blackbird!**

She wasn't talking to the blackbird like she usually talks to birds . . .

Grandma was talking to the blackbird as if they were **old friends** having a chat!

'Grandma, **what are you doing?**' I asked.

The blackbird cheeped loudly and Grandma laughed. 'That's very funny, Terry,' she said back to him.

Terry?!

'You call the blackbird Terry?'

I asked.

'Of course! Because that's his name!' Grandma replied. 'Have a chat to him, Nelson. He's a fascinating fella,' she said. 'Oh, you'll need this.'

I didn't know what to think as Grandma took the helmet off and put it on **my head!**

As soon as the helmet was on, I could hear the blackbird talking to me. Not in **bird cheeps** . . . but **IN ENGLISH!**

You look weird in that helmet, dude!

I was so shocked, I **ripped** the helmet off my head!

'What's wrong?' Grandma asked. 'Don't you like my new invention?'

'You can make animals **talk?!'**

'Of course not! They **already know** how to talk. The helmet translates their language into English, and what we say into their language.'

'That's **AMAZING!'**

Kenny put on the helmet and started talking to a **lizard!**

'This is your **COOLEST** invention ever, Grandma!' Kenny said.

'I'm glad you think so,' Grandma replied. 'Because I've made one for each of you!'

WOOHOO!

As she placed the two helmets on the bench, the top of one fell off.

'Oops!' said Grandma. 'A bit of tape will fix that. I'll fix it now, while you're hanging out with your friend.'

She pointed to **Tiffany** who was skipping towards the junkyard.

'Tiffany's **early** for our **circus rehearsal!**' Kenny said, panicking. 'I need to get changed. She can't see me like this!'

'She sees you dressed like that every day!' I said.

But Kenny was already scurrying back inside.

'What's this about a circus rehearsal?' Grandma asked.

'One lucky act will get to perform with the **SHAW FAMILY CIRCUS,**' I explained.

'How exciting!' Grandma said. 'Did you know, before your dad developed his ninja skills, he wanted to join the circus.'

'Really?!' I asked. I loved hearing about my dad.

'He used to spend hours **juggling, balancing** on a tightrope and trying to ride a unicycle. Sometimes all at once!'

'Was Dad good at circus tricks?' I asked.

'No!' Grandma laughed. 'He was terrible! Before he became a ninja, he had no balance or co-ordination at all!'

'Just like me!' I exclaimed.

'Exactly like you!' Grandma laughed.

Grandma's face became more serious. 'Nelson, you need to make sure you **don't** use any of your **ninja skills** during your circus audition.'

'Why does it matter so much if people know I'm **NINJA KID**?'

'If Dr Kane finds out your **true identity**, you could be in real **danger**,' replied Grandma. 'And so could those **around you**.'

'But we haven't seen Dr Kane in **ages**!' I replied.

'That's what I'm worried about,' Grandma said.

Grandma waved to Tiffany as she arrived. 'Hello, Tiffany. I'll leave you kids to it!' She tottered off.

'Where's Kenny?' Tiffany asked.

'Ah, he wanted to change into something more comfortable for our rehearsal,' I replied.

'I love his enthusiasm!' Tiffany beamed.

But when Kenny returned in his **new outfit,** he didn't look comfortable at all!

'Yo, Tiffany, what's happening?' Kenny asked. For some reason he was trying to act really **COOL!**

'That's an . . . **interesting** . . . rehearsal outfit,' Tiffany said.

'Glad you **dig it,**' Kenny said.

'Dig it?' Tiffany looked confused.

'Tiffany, can you excuse us for a second,' I said, dragging Kenny away.

'Help yourself to one of my high-protein energy bars!' Kenny called.

'Kenny, you're acting **super weird**,' I whispered.

'Tiffany's cool,' Kenny said, 'so if I want her to be my friend, I have to **pretend to be cool**, too.'

'You don't have to pretend to be anything,' I said. 'Tiffany likes you for who you are.'

'You don't know anything about what girls like,' Kenny said.

He did have a point.

Then he strutted back to Tiffany as if he was a **ROCK STAR!**

'So, what's our circus act going to be?' I asked.

'Something **COOL!**' Kenny said.

'Something **FUNNY!**' Tiffany said.

'I have no idea what's **COOL** or **FUNNY** . . .' I said. 'But maybe we should try **juggling.** How hard can that be?'

We started practising with **balls** . . .

Then we tried juggling **clubs** . . .

Then we tried with **rings** . . .

'We should play to our **strengths**,' I said.

'I do **gymnastics**,' Tiffany said. 'Maybe we can work out an **acrobatic routine?**'

'Excellent idea!' I said. 'What do you think, Kenny?'

But Kenny was racing back to the house.

When Kenny returned, he was wearing **another** bizarre outfit!

Thanks to Tiffany's awesome gymnastic skills we soon came up with a great routine.

Kenny and I balanced a beam while Tiffany did **AMAZING MOVES** on top of it, including handstands, cartwheels and **backbends . . .**

I was proud of myself for not revealing my **ninja powers** the whole time we'd been practising . . . until Tiffany **fell** off the beam.

I did a **flip** and a **roll** and **caught** her just before she hit the ground!

Tiffany stared at me in disbelief. '**How did you do that?**'

Kenny answered for me. 'Because he's a ninj-mmmmm . . .'

I had to shove a protein bar into Kenny's mouth to stop him **giving away** my secret identity!

I've lost track of how many times Kenny has almost blurted out that I'm **Ninja Kid.**

While he was munching away, I tried to come up with something to explain myself to Tiffany.

'Well, we'll need more than beginner's luck on the day of the auditions. Let's keep practising!' said Tiffany.

THREE

By the time the auditions came around, Kenny, Tiffany and I had practised our routine **Soooo many times.** We thought we could even do it with our **eyes closed** . . . but that wasn't a good idea!

BUMP!

'I'm proud of you boys for **practising** so hard,' Grandma said as we ate breakfast.

'Your dad would be especially **proud,** Nelson,' Mum said. 'Did you know he wanted to start a family circus?'

'Wow!' I said. 'That would have been so cool.'

'Now it's up to the two of you to represent the family,' Mum said.

Even though we had our routine totally sorted, we were still **nervous.** We knew everyone else in our class had been practising really hard, too. And it wasn't just school kids who were trying out. **Everyone in town** was invited to audition!

When we got to school, the gym was **full** of people waiting to strut their stuff.

We knew Charles and Sarah had been practising a lot because Charles wouldn't stop talking about it. 'My dad said that Sarah and I are better than most professional magicians - including the Amazing Allison!' he told everyone.

The **AMAZING ALLISON** was the most famous magician in the world. She once made the Eiffel Tower disappear!

Sarah was embarrassed by Charles's boasting.

The judges for the circus tryouts were **BING** and **ZING**, two brothers who were **trapeze artists** from the **SHAW FAMILY CIRCUS.**

'Who among you is brave enough to audition **first?'** Bing asked.

The only people to put their hands up were **Billy Bob** and his partner, Daisy.

'Come up and introduce yourselves,' Zing said.

'We're the **LASSO LEGENDS**, and we can lasso anything!' Billy Bob said excitedly.

'Let's see it!' said Bing.

First, they tried to lasso some chairs . . . but Billy Bob just lassoed himself!

Next, they tried to catch cartons of milk in their lassos . . .

but they just ended up splashing milk all over everyone at the front of the gym!

'OK! I think we've seen enough of the **lasso legends!**' Bing said.

'Give them a round of applause, everybody!' Zing added.

We all clapped and Billy Bob and Daisy did a little **jig** as they left the stage.

'OK, who's next?' Bing asked.

There were lots of great auditions. Mr Fletcher sang a duet with his pet pug, Poppy!

Ms Quick did a **plate-spinning act** where she kept five plates spinning on a stick with her incredible speed.

Finally, it was time for us to do our routine. We called ourselves the **GLEESOME THREESOME!**

Performing in front of Bing, Zing and the big crowd made me super nervous. But somehow Kenny and I managed to hold the beam still while Tiffany did an

Then she did **backbends . . .**

Then she did a **cartwheel!**

The crowd **clapped** and **cheered.**

'That was **brilliant!'** Bing said.

'Give it up for the Gleesome Threesome!' Zing cheered.

It felt amazing to pull off the routine! As we sat back down, Sarah gave us a **double thumbs up.**

'Who do we have next?' asked Zing.

Sarah and Charles were just about to walk up to the stage when there was an enormous **rumbling** outside the gym.

It was getting **louder and louder . . .**

until . . .

CRASH!

FOUR

Bursting through the doors was the **biggest rhino** any of us had ever seen! And the man riding him had the **biggest black beard** we'd ever seen!

'I am **Rocco!**' the man boomed. 'And this is my beautiful rhino, **Rita.**'

Rita's **ROAR** was **so loud** it **shook** the floor of the gym.

'We're here to audition for the circus!' said Rocco.

'Then **step right up!**' Bing replied.

'But don't **step on** anybody!' Zing added.

Rocco and Rita **STOMPED** up onto the stage.

Rocco jumped off Rita, **clapped** his hands and yelled, '**MUSIC!**'

A **hip-hop** song began blasting out from **Rocco's hat.** Then Rita rose up on two feet and started **breakdancing!** It was unbelievable!

Rita **crumped** . . .

Rita did headspins,

the electric boogaloo,

and even the caterpillar!

Rita could do anything a human hip-hop dancer could do, even though she was fifty times **HEAVIER!**

We all **clapped** and **cheered** and **hooted.**

'This is the **BEST** thing I've ever seen!' Tiffany said.

'Totally totes!' Kenny said. He was still trying to act cool!

'Kenny, please stop trying to be cool,' Tiffany said. 'I don't care about cool! I like people who are funny and kind.'

'Great news!' Kenny said. 'Because I am funny and kind . . . and sometimes **both at the same time!'** Kenny said.

'I know!' Tiffany said.

'For our next trick, I need a **volunteer!'** Rocco called out to the crowd.

'Me! Me!' shouted Charles. He was already bounding onto the stage, ignoring all the other kids with their hands up.

'Make sure you save some **energy** for our routine,' Sarah called to him.

'I don't care about our **stupid routine** anymore!' Charles said. 'I'm all about the **MEGA RHINO!'**

I could see Sarah was upset, so Kenny, Tiffany and I moved up to sit next to her.

'What's your name?' asked Rocco.

'Charles Brock!' said Charles proudly.

'Now, Charles Brock, Rita and I need you to stand very **still**.'

'BORING!' Charles replied.

'You might not find it boring when Rita the Rhino **does a triple front flip over your head!'**

'Drum roll please!' Rocco yelled. A drum roll burst from Rocco's hat. 'Rita the Rhino, are you ready?'

Rita **ROARED.**

'Charles Brock, are you ready?'

'Not really!' Charles replied. His legs were **wobbling** like jelly.

I was beginning to feel worried. Sure, Charles could be mean, but I didn't want him to get **crushed** by a giant rhino!

The crowd was silent.

Suddenly, Rocco **clapped** . . .

Rita the Rhino leapt into the air and did the most **awesome flip** over Charles's head.

Everyone in the crowd went **absolutely NUTS!** They all jumped to their feet and started **chanting,**

'RITA! RITA! RITA!'

Sarah was such a good sport that she clapped and chanted, too.

Bing and Zing returned to the stage.

'WOW!' said Bing.

'Super wow!' said Zing. 'It's going to be very difficult to top that act!'

'Impossible!' Bing added. 'Does anyone else want to audition?'

Charles was now too busy **posing** with Rita and Rocco to bother doing his act with Sarah. She looked really upset.

'Sarah, if you still want to audition, I could help you with your routine? If you want . . .' I said.

Sarah smiled at me. 'Really? That would be great! All you have to do is lie down. Can you do that?'

'I'm **awesome** at lying down!' I said.

Sarah **thrust** her hand in the air and Bing and Zing called us up to the stage.

'Ladies and gentlemen, I am **SARAH THE SORCERER**,' Sarah announced. 'And today I am going to cut my good friend Nelson in half!'

Whaaaaat?!

'Lovely Nelson, if you could lie in the **Box of Death** please,' Sarah said.

BOX OF DEATH?!

What had I got myself into?

'Don't worry,' whispered Sarah. 'I know what I'm doing.'

'I'm glad one of us does . . .' I whispered back.

Sarah wheeled the Box of Death onto the stage and I climbed inside.

'Don't move a muscle,' Sarah whispered.

'I don't think I could even if I wanted to!' I replied. The box was really **small**!

Sarah spun the box around three times, and then produced a **HUGE saw.**

'Are you ready to be a half-Nelson?' she said to me.

Sarah started sawing the box in half. I clenched my eyes shut. I was terrified!

Next thing I knew, the crowd was cheering. I opened my eyes and couldn't believe it.

'What do you think, everyone, should I put Nelson back together? He looks more **handsome** in one piece!'

I blushed so much my face turned as red as a strawberry!

The crowd all cheered. Sarah spun the boxes around, joined them back together, and opened the lid.

I was back in one piece!

TADA!

The full Nelson!

The crowd **cheered** loudly again.

As we walked off stage, Sarah was **beaming.** 'That was so much fun! Thanks, Nelson!'

'Thanks for not actually sawing me in half. And for calling me handsome!'

Sarah laughed. 'That was just for show!' she said.

'So how did you do it?' I asked.

'Not telling! It's a **MAGIC TRICK!**' Sarah replied.

We sat back down next to Kenny and Tiffany.

'Sensational sorcering, Sarah!' Tiffany said.

Kenny looked really worried. 'Do you need a **bandaid?** Or twenty?' he asked me. He thought Sarah really had sawn me in half and put me back together!

Zing and Bing returned to the stage.

'Alright, circus stars, time to announce a winner,' Zing said excitedly. 'Bing and I both agree that the standard today was very **high.** Give yourselves a huge round of **applause.**'

'But there was **one act** that stood head and shoulders above the rest . . .

Rocco and his fabulous breakdancing rhino, Rita!' Bing said.

'Thank you! Thank you!' Rocco boomed. 'See you all at the circus!'

Rocco jumped on Rita's back and they thundered out of the gym.

THUMP! THUMP! THUMP!

No-one could argue with Bing and Zing's decision. Rocco and Rita were incredible. We couldn't wait to see them again at the circus!

FiVE

On the morning of the excursion, Mum and Grandma were **excited for us.**

'Wish I could come with you!' Mum said.

'Me too!' Grandma added.

Mum gave me and Kenny **some money** to buy a snack.

'I'll be too amazed watching the circus to need snacks,' Kenny said.

'And **pigs might fly!'** Grandma joked.

'Take these with you, too, boys,' Grandma said, handing us our **animal translation helmets.**

'Why would we need these on a circus excursion?'

‘So you can chat to Rita the Rhino and the other circus animals,’ Grandma said. But I could tell by the way Grandma looked at me that there was more to it than that.

We stuffed the helmets into our bags and Mum dropped us at school. As Kenny and I queued for the bus, Kenny looked really **worried.**

'Are you worried you'll get **bus-sick** again?' I asked.

On the way home from the Planetarium excursion, Kenny turned so green he looked like an **avocado!**

'No,' Kenny said. 'I only get bus-sick when I eat two bags of chilli chips and drink a chocolate milk right before I get on the bus!'

But he was **sweating** like crazy.

'Nelson, I'm not sure how to say this so I'm just going to **blurt** it out . . . Tiffany asked me if I'd sit next to her on the bus . . . and I said yes.'

'That's cool,' I replied.

I was really happy for Kenny, but I knew my bus ride would now be a lot less fun. I'd probably have to sit next to **Charles Brock** or one of the teachers.

As I got on the bus a familiar voice called out, 'Saved you a seat, Nelson!'

It was Sarah!

On the way to the circus, Sarah and I had our best chat ever. We didn't just talk about all the stuff we **liked,** we talked about things that made us **upset,** too.

Sarah told me that her parents had **separated.**

And I told Sarah about how my dad went missing, and I hadn't seen him since I was really young.

I wanted to tell Sarah all about how I was **Ninja Kid,** too. But then I remembered what Grandma told me . . .

If Dr Kane finds out your true identity, you could be in real danger. And so could those around you . . .

So I quickly changed the topic to Rita the Rhino instead.

Kenny and Tiffany spent the whole bus ride talking about **food!** Turns out they loved eating all the same things!

YUM!

They both even lick the cream off a biscuit before eating the outside!

Talking to Sarah made the bus trip go super quickly and before I knew it, we were there!

The **BIG TOP** was packed!

Talking to Tiffany had made Kenny really hungry. He added some of his own **pocket money** to the money Mum gave us for snacks and almost bought the **whole candy bar!**

Even though Kenny loved food he was awesome at **sharing.** He bought us all a **choc-top** and a box of **popcorn.** And Tiffany and Kenny both ate **all** the chocolate off their choc-top before eating the ice-cream!

We were all buzzing with excitement when the **ringmaster** stepped onto the stage. He was wearing a red velvet suit and had an amazing **TWIRLY moustache.**

'I am your ringmaster, **Colonel Shaw,** and I'm very proud to introduce our first act - my two **incredibly talented** children . . . **Bing** and **Zing!**

Bing and Zing were the most amazing **trapeze artists.** We gasped as they did **flips, spins** and **leaps** high above us.

The next act was just as jaw dropping - **performing poodles!** They could **prance, dance** and

go

down

a

slide!

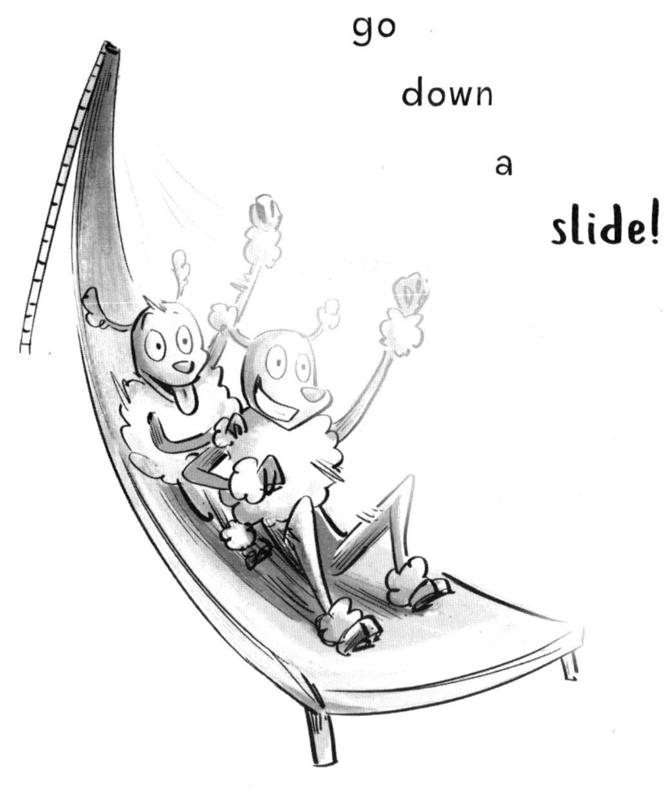

They weren't the only **amazing performing animals.**

The Shaw Family Circus had **singing horses!**

BOING!

There were **trampolining goats!**

As well as doing tricks on the trampoline, the goats could **faint** on cue!

There were also **ping-pong playing pigs!**

And two beautiful **macaws** that could play **basketball!** One of them could even **dunk!**

Then there was the **Wheel of Steel!** Three **motorbike riders** screeched around a small cage while Bing and Zing stood in the middle.

And there was **Hannah the Hula Hooper.** She spun so many **hula hoops** we couldn't see her!

This really was the best circus ever!

SiX

Then, the moment we'd been waiting for finally arrived. The ringmaster stepped forward and announced, 'It is time for our local competition winners to perform!'

We all cheered loudly as **Rocco and Rita** made their way up to the stage.

THUMP! THUMP!

'What are you **feeding** that rhino?' the ringmaster asked Rocco.

Everybody laughed, but Rocco wasn't amused. 'None of your business,' he snapped. He seemed a lot **less friendly** today.

Rocco called for Charles to join them again and Charles ran up to the stage like **he'd** just won a competition!

His dad, Mayor Brock, called out from the VIP seats, 'Show them who's boss, Charles!'

Rocco clapped and shouted, '*Ballet!*'

This time, it wasn't **hip-hop** music that blasted out of his hat, it was classical music! And Rita didn't front flip over Charles . . . she danced with him as if they were in the **Royal Ballet!**

You could tell Charles was **embarrassed,** but we all thought it was **fantastic!**

We **whooped** and **clapped** even louder than last time.

After the dance, as Charles returned to his seat, he **pumped** his fists in the air as if he was the **star** of the show!

'And now for our next trick . . .' Rocco announced. He nodded at Rita.

The giant rhino **roared** loudly.

Then there was a huge **FLAP, FLAP, FLAP** above the **BIG TOP.** The sound was almost deafening . . .

A **giant flying WARTHOG** came bursting through the Big Top roof!

'My precious **BIG TOP!'** the ringmaster cried as the flying warthog joined Rita and Rocco on stage.

The warthog was one of the **scariest** things I'd ever seen. It had **gnashing** teeth, **gnarly** tusks and **giant** black wings.

'Wow! Pigs really can fly!' Kenny exclaimed.

Then we heard **another loud flapping** noise coming from above.

'Oh, man, what's next?' Kenny asked. 'A flying goat?'

But it was even crazier than that . . .

It was a

FLYING HIPPO!

'This is starting to get **CREEPY**,' Sarah said.

'**Super** creepy,' Tiffany agreed.

Rita the Rhino reared up on two legs and then **huge wings** sprouted out of her back!

The vibe inside the Big Top had changed from **excitement** to **fear.** People started scurrying out of the Big Top.

Rocco watched on from the stage, **laughing** loudly. Then he ripped off his **hat** and his **beard . . .**

IT WAS DR KANE!

'I knew there was something **familiar** about that dude,' Kenny said.

'Then why didn't you say something?' I asked.

'Because I thought he was the owner of the local fish and chip shop!'

'I'm not just **taking over** this circus!' Dr Kane boomed. 'I am taking over this **town!**'

'No, you're not!' the ringmaster said, rushing onto the stage. 'Don't fear, everybody, I have worked with animals all my life. I'll calm these **bad-tempered beasts.**'

Then the ringmaster spoke to the flying animals as if he were talking to the performing poodles . . .

But the animals completely **ignored** him.

Dr Kane **howled** with laughter. 'They're not real animals, you fool!' he scoffed. 'These are my latest **creations!** I have spent years designing these **beautiful ROBOTIC beasts.**'

'Beautiful?!' Kenny exclaimed.

'Everyone has different taste,' Tiffany shrugged.

'And the hippo is sort of cute . . . in a **giant-mechanical-flying-animal** kind of way,' Sarah said.

Sarah always tried to see the good side in everything - even **EVIL ROBOTIC** hippos!

Dr Kane **snatched** the megaphone off the ringmaster, jumped onto Rita's back and **soared** above us. The other two beasts followed.

HAHAHA!

'Unless you want to be **pulverised** by my **winged warriors,** I suggest you all leave Duck Creek immediately!'

Dr Kane yelled.

Someone had to do something . . . and

FAST!

SEVEN

If **NINJA KID** and **H-DUDE** didn't make an appearance soon, Dr Kane would scare **everyone** out of Duck Creek.

But we couldn't just **put our disguises on** in front of everyone and reveal our **secret identities!**

I knew it would look bad if we ran off, but we had no choice.

'Ah, I need to go to the toilet!' I said.

'Me too!' Kenny added.

'NOW?!' Tiffany exclaimed.

'**Both** of you?!' Sarah said.

'Flying robotic creatures always make me want to pee!' Kenny added.

Tiffany and Sarah looked totally shocked as we **rushed off.**

As we turned the corner, we saw the giant flying warthog . . . coming straight for us!

'Stop, drop and roll!' Kenny yelled.

We dropped to the ground and the warthog swooped over the top of us.

We hurried into the bathroom. Luckily there was no-one in there.

We quickly got changed and stepped back out.

All the kids **cheered** when they saw Ninja Kid and H-Dude were on the scene.

We knew defeating Dr Kane's robotic beasts would be hard, but then I remembered we had a **secret weapon** . . .

GRANDMA'S ANIMAL TRANSLATION HELMETS!

I rushed over to the **horses** while Kenny went to find the performing **poodles.**

The horses had been spooked by the flying animals and when I walked towards them, they **whinnied** angrily.

I set the helmet settings to **HORSE.**

'It's OK,' I said through the helmet. 'I'm Ninja Kid. I'm not going to hurt you.'

The horses were **stunned** that I could speak their language!

'My name is **HERCULES**,' replied one of the horses. Even though he was the smallest, he had an incredibly deep voice!

'We're going to need your help to stop these robots,' I said.

'But we're **singers,** not fighters!' Hercules said. 'And we can't fly.'

'You don't need to fight, or fly,' I said. 'But you can help **me** do a little bit of both!'

'We'll help you!' Hercules said.

Kenny had also convinced the performing poodles to help us.

'OK, poodle pals, **let's go!'** he yelled above the awful roaring of the robotic monsters.

Kenny and I were just about to put our plan into practice when I had a last-minute thought. 'H-Dude, come with me!'

We raced over to Sarah and Tiffany.

'We were wondering if you two might be able to help us?' I asked.

'Of course, Ninja Kid!' Sarah said.

'Nice to see you again, H-Dude!' Tiffany said. 'What do you need us to do?'

'This is going to sound a little crazy,' I said. 'But these helmets let you talk to animals . . .'

Sarah and Tiffany looked at us like we were **bonkers!**

'The horses and the poodles are already helping us,' Kenny explained.

'So if you can talk to the macaws, the goats and the pigs, we might be able to stop these **ROBOTIC ANIMALS** from taking over Duck Creek. You just have to set the language to whichever animal you're talking to.'

'Ah . . . OK,' Sarah said.

Sarah and Tiffany grabbed the **helmets** and Kenny and I raced back to the horses and poodles.

Kenny stood on the large mat underneath the trapeze bars. 'Let's do this!' he yelled.

The poodles all stood up on **two legs**, grabbed hold of the mat and **launched** Kenny into the air. He soared high and landed on the back of the **flying hippo!**

The hippo was **not happy** about Kenny being on his back and tried to buck him off . . .

Somehow, Kenny managed to hold on and stop the hippo swooping over the crowd.

Then it was **my** turn.

As the flying warthog soared towards me, I called out, **'Giddy-up!'**

Two horses flicked me high into the air . . .

and I landed on top of the **warthog!**

The mechanical animals tried to throw us off, but Kenny and I both held on tight.

'This isn't as fun as I thought it would be!' Kenny yelled.

'You thought riding an angry flying hippo would be **FUN?!'** I shouted back.

We were trying to steer the animals to the ground but they weren't obeying.

'C'mon, Mr Hippo, time for a rest!' Kenny said. The flying hippo **bucked** him so hard he almost dropped to the ground. Dr Kane **laughed.**

Things weren't going well.

Luckily, we still had Sarah, Tiffany and their **animal army** to help us.

Sarah convinced the goats to form a **pyramid** in the middle of the stage.

It was a pretty impressive sight!

The two **macaws** flew to the very top of the goat pyramid and called out to the hippo.

'Yeah, come on, big boy, BRING IT!' the second macaw chimed in.

'Your wish is my command!' Dr Kane yelled.

The hippo nodded and flew straight towards the **goat pyramid.** Oh no! He was going to crash into our new friends!

But then, all of a sudden, the goats pretended to **faint!** It was only then I realised they had been standing right in front of the **Wheel of Steel.**

Kenny jumped off the flying hippo just before it flew inside.

Sarah quickly **slammed** the door, locking the giant hippo inside.

The flying hippo rammed into the sides of the Wheel of Steel, trying to escape.

But it was no use, the steel cage was too strong. Eventually, the robotic hippo ran out of power and lay down.

Dr Kane was **fuming.** 'You'll pay for that Ninja Kid and H-Dude!' Then he turned to Rita and the flying warthog.

'ATTACK!'

The robot animals started to dive towards the ground.

ARRGGHH!

I looked down and saw the ping-pong playing pigs had formed a huddle, with their ping-pong paddles raised in combat.

As we flew past the trapeze, I **leapt off** and reached out to grab it . . .

and missed!

But Bing and Zing were there to catch me!

As the warthog flew towards them, Tiffany and the pigs started throwing **hula hoop** after **hula hoop**.

The warthog **thrashed** and **bashed,** trying to break free of the hula hoops, but there were too many of them. It **thumped** to the ground and eventually ran out of power, too.

'My beautiful beasts!' Dr Kane yelled, distraught.

He turned to his beloved rhino, Rita, the **biggest** and **strongest** of his mechanical creatures.

FINISH THEM!

EiGHT

Rita the Rhino snorted and flew towards the roof. At first I thought she was making an **escape**.

But then she

turned . . .

and came **spearing** straight for us!

The horses and pigs bolted out of the way and all the goats fainted. For real this time!

We were about to be **crunched.** I had to think quickly. Next to us was one of the giant **poles** that propped up the Big Top.

'When I give the signal, everyone jump behind the pole,' I told the others.

We all jumped behind the pole just seconds before the rhino **crashed** into it.

SMASH!

The whole Big Top **shook!** But Rita the Rhino barely flinched.

'Nice try!' Dr Kane shouted. 'Rita's body is made of **TITANIUM.** A little pole can't hurt her!'

But the collision **did** break off a part of Rita's **horn.** I expected to see lots of **wiring** inside Rita's robotic head but instead . . .

there was a **CHIPMUNK** sitting inside!

It was the **same** chipmunk Kenny had zapped with the **SWITCHEROO MACHINE** at our athletics carnival!

'This doesn't make sense!' Kenny said. 'I thought their brains were switched?!'

'I know!' I replied. 'If Dr Kane is back to normal, how can the chipmunk still be smart enough to control a mechanical animal?'

'You have a **sidekick,** Ninja Kid, so I decided to keep this little guy as mine!' Dr Kane bellowed. 'This is **EINSTEIN THE CHIPMUNK** and I've made him **smarter** than any human being.'

'That's right, **dumb dumbs!** My intelligence is extraordinary!' Einstein laughed. 'It's been fun, Ninja Kid and H-Dude, but now it's time for you two **clowns** to take a **final bow!**'

He **cranked** up the speed and steered the rhino straight towards us.

There was **no way** we could overpower a robot rhino! And **no way** we could outsmart **Einstein!**

But then I had one last idea . . .

'Music!' I shouted.

Just as I'd hoped, hip-hop music started playing from Dr Kane's hat. And instead of ramming into us, Rita the Rhino immediately landed on the ground and started

breakdancing!

Dr Kane was furious. **'Music off! MUSIC OFF!'** he shouted at his hat.

The music stopped . . . but Rita kept dancing! She was busting some amazing moves!

'NO, NO, NO!' Dr Kane bellowed. 'Einstein! What are YOU DOING?!'

Einstein poked his head out of the robotic rhino. 'I can't control her anymore! It's like Rita has a mind of her own.'

'That's ridiculous!' Dr Kane said. 'She is a **ROBOT!**'

But Einstein had bigger things to worry about - Rita was preparing to do **THE WORM!**

'Abandon mission!' Dr Kane cried out.

'Agreed!' Einstein said. He disappeared inside the rhino. A few seconds later, a miniature **helicopter** flew out . . . of the

rhino's

behind!

A long **ladder** dropped down from the mini-chopper and Dr Kane climbed onto it. Somehow, the tiny helicopter **lifted** Dr Kane off the ground and it headed towards the broken roof!

'I'll get you next time, Ninja Kid!' Dr Kane called down to us.

'I'll get you even **worse!**' Einstein added.

Then they flew through the hole in the **BIG TOP** and out of sight.

Those still left in the crowd **cheered** loudly for us.

Kenny called out, 'Can we also get a big round of applause for our awesome animal friends: the performing poodles, the cheeky macaws, the singing horses, the ping-pong pigs and the amazing fainting goats!'

All the animals came out to take a bow!

While everyone was taking **photos** of the animals, Kenny and I **snuck** into the bathroom and changed. By the time we found Sarah and Tiffany again, the animals had all left the stage and the ringmaster was sweeping up.

'Where have you been?' Sarah asked.

'You missed **EVERYTHING!**' Tiffany added.

'Um, there was a **HUGE** queue for the toilets!' I said.

'Looks like someone tamed those nasty robotic animals while we were gone!' Kenny added.

'It was **Ninja Kid** and **H-Dude**!' Tiffany said. 'They were **AMAZING!**'

'You miss them every time!' Sarah said.

'Shame!' said Kenny. 'They sound really **cool!**'

'Yeah, **H-Dude** is the best!' Tiffany said. 'But I'm-mmm . . .'

I stuffed a juggling ball into Kenny's mouth so he wouldn't reveal his identity!

Because Sarah and Tiffany thought we had missed everything, they **told us about** every second of the action on the bus ride home.

NiNE

That night, we told Mum and Grandma all about our **crazy** circus day.

'We would've been in big trouble without the animal translation helmets,' Kenny said.

'You knew we'd need it, didn't you, Grandma?' I asked.

'Your dad and your uncle have always **loved** animals and the circus,' Grandma said. 'It's a tragedy that your Uncle Andrew's love has turned into hate.'

'Do you think we'll ever see Dad again?' I asked.

'I wish I knew,' Grandma replied.

'I hope so,' said Mum. 'But what we do know is that he would be so **proud** of you boys,' she added. 'Not just for saving the day, but for putting on a one-show only **KANE FAMILY CIRCUS!**'

READ THEM ALL!

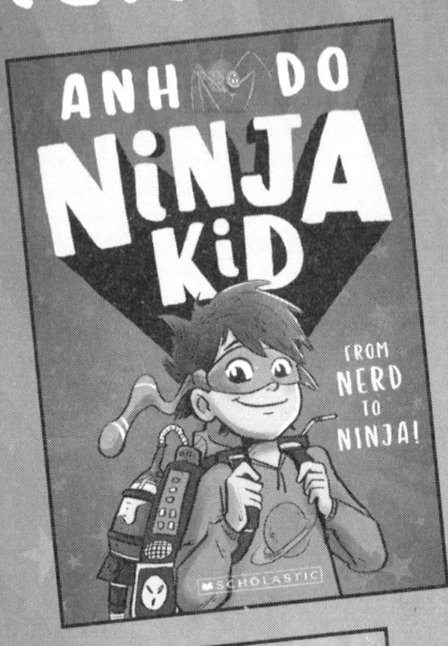

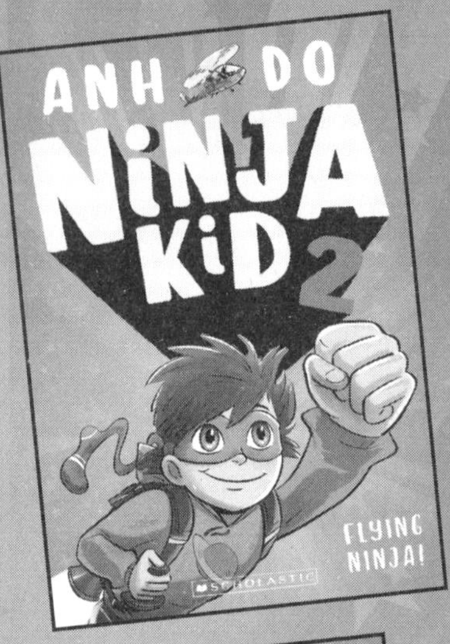

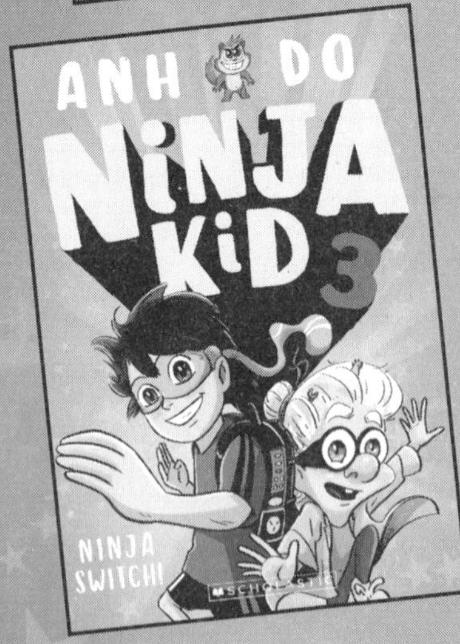

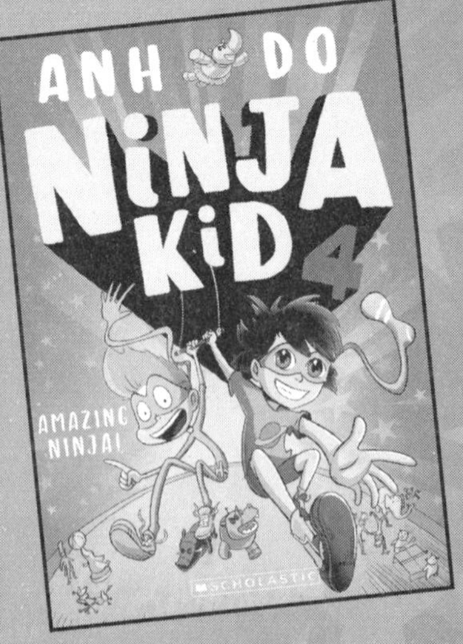

NINJA KID 5 COMING SOON!